Listen

HOW TO BE YOU IN A WORLD WHERE YOU CAN BE ANYTHING

LISTEN MORE. DO LESS. BECOME EXTRAORDINARY.

Ryan Fahey

Listen: How To Be You In A World Where You Can Be Anything © Copyright 2023 Ryan B Fahey All rights reserved. No part of this publication may be reproduced, distributed, or transmitted in any form or by any means, including phocopying, recording, or other electronic or mechanical methods, without the prior written permission of the publisher, except in the case of brief quotations embodied in critical reviews and certain other noncommercial uses permitted by copyright law.

Although the author and publisher have made every effort to ensure that the information in this book was correct at press time, the author and publisher do not assume and hereby disclaim any liability to any party for any loss, damage, or disruption caused by errors or omissions, whether such errors or omissions result from negligence, accident, or any other cause.

Adherence to all applicable laws and regulations, including international, federal, state and local governing professional licensing, business practices, advertising, and all other aspects of doing business in the US, Canada or any other jurisdiction is the sole responsibility of the reader and consumer.

Neither the author nor the publisher assumes any responsibility or liability whatsoever on behalf of the consumer or reader of this material. Any perceived slight of any individual or organization is purely unintentional.

The resources in this book are provided for informational purposes only and should not be used to replace the specialized training and professional judgment of a health care

or mental health care professional.

Neither the author nor the publisher can be held responsible for the use of the information provided within this book. Please always consult a trained professional before making any decision regarding the treatment of yourself or others.

For more information, email faheyconsulting@gmail.com.

ISBN: 978-1-7776861-6-1

TABLE OF CONTENTS

Foreword 1
Introduction 5

Chapter 1
The Age of Fluidity 9

Chapter 2
The Bottomless Economy 15

Chapter 3
Professional Awareness and Building Wealth 21

Chapter 4
Happiness 27

Chapter 5
1 Year Early Or 1 Minute Late 39

Chapter 6
Swim With The Tide 74

Chapter 7
Cautiously Seeking Advice 53

Chapter 8
Trust and Preparation 59

Chapter 9
Embracing The Fallow Season 66

Chapter 10
Lightning In and Around The Bottle 72

Conclusion 80

Career and Life Book Recommendations 82

Endnotes 83

ENDORSEMENTS

"Through transformative insights, Ryan's book urges readers to trust their instincts, navigate change, and embrace fulfillment. Filled with invaluable wisdom, it's a must-read for anyone seeking genuine happiness and lasting success. A profound reminder to listen more, do less, and become extraordinary."

Heather Moyse - Motivational Keynote Speaker, Coach, Author of *Redefining 'Realistic'*, 2x Olympic Gold Medalist

"Ryan's book encourages us to ask the deep questions we avoid, with the reward of living more authentically. I highly recommend this book to anyone courageous enough to believe there's more to life."

Sam Demma - Keynote Speaker and Bestselling Author

"If you only had one success blueprint to follow, grab this one! Ryan has distilled the best actionable guide to mastering yourself based on proven strategies throughout the ages. Forget all the books you haven't read yet. Ryan has already read them and distilled them for you here. An excellent, simple read."

Jeff Dolan - CEO of Wavve

"Ryan captures your attention with his stellar storytelling ability. His ability to synthesize the wisdom and expertise of well known authors is second to none. His book prompted me to rethink how I view wealth and moved me to reflect on how I truly want to show up in my life.

To strengthen your resolve to "BE YOU" in a world where you can be anything, I highly recommend this book!"

Joyce Sunada - Wellness Educator, Keynote Speaker, Workshop Facilitator & Wellness Coach

Other Publications By Ryan Fahey

Thought Leadership: How Great Thinking Produces Life-long Wealth
Your Best Decade
Your Best Journal
How To Thrive In Remote Working Environments

Additional Online Publications Can Be Found On:

The StartUp
Data Driven Investor
Fit Biz Weekly Magazine
The Good Men Project
The Canadian Way

FOREWORD

Are you chasing happiness? Wealth? Stability? Satisfaction? What will it look and feel like when you get there? If you are busy overthinking your answer... Take a breath.

Listen, in an era saturated with voices instructing us to be <u>something</u>, achieve everything, get rich now, and aspire constantly, it's easy to overlook the singular voice of reason we should be prioritizing: our own. *Listen: How to Be You in a World Where You Can Be Anything* isn't just another guide; it's a transformative manual for living life well.

This book reminds us to slow down to move forward, and Ryan brilliantly weaves a cautionary tale of a world where the noise makes it impossible for us to know what we really want and need. His road map for finding our sense of curiosity, courage, and agility in a world where we can do anything reminds us that life has many backroads that we have never navigated.

Ryan's work moves us away from a world of convenience, instant gratification, and fleeting satisfactions, driving us towards the real wealth, pride, and fulfillment that comes from carving our own path and molding a life with values and purpose.

Ryan helps you stay nimble and curious, with the ability to focus on what is most important by stopping, decluttering your mind and your world.

If hesitation is your guide and fear is your compass for making decisions because there are just too many answers, this is the book for you.

In 2013, I met an extraordinary individual. From the moment you encounter Ryan Fahey, you are pulled into his charismatic enthusiasm for connection, ingenuity, and a zest for life. He has a unique gift: in a mere instant, he made me feel as though my story, my identity, and my voice were the most valuable in the room. His profound experience in education, entrepreneurship, personal growth, and well-being forms the foundation of his persona and the wisdom he imparts on the world.

A decade later, I sought his guidance and expertise, trusting him with my most cherished stories and concepts, and he helped me navigate my first book , *Return To Play: Rebuilding Resilience, Risk, and Reconnection*, now a best-seller in Inclusive Education and Educational Leadership.

Having committed over two decades to adult education, inclusion, and therapeutic play, I can vehemently vouch for the significant need for people of all walks of life to stop long enough to live your life on purpose. Ryan's work propels us to escape the shackles of constant contemplation and apprehension (that little voice that holds us back from trying something new or doing what our heart knows is right). His insights and wisdom pave the way to rediscover our inherent curiosity, bravery, and adaptability – the attributes that empower us to maneuver through life's unpredictable terrains with courage and confidence.

Today's world, ever obsessed with the next big thing, constantly faces monumental challenges. This frenetic pace has eroded our innate ability to be curious, to pause, and to approach the unfamiliar with wonder rather than dread. But it shouldn't be that way.

At the beginning of this book, Ryan poses an important question: "Who are you becoming really?" I remember reading it over and over, and considering all the ways we avoid the "really". So many of us can state our intentions, values, and goals, but the "really" asks us to take off all the filters and masks, the should be and have to be, the Instagram posts and false narratives, and get real with ourselves.

Our world is plagued with decision fatigue, where the sheer magnitude of available choices can immobilize us. Over-customization leads to immobilization. We simply don't know what to do when presented with all the options. This book gracefully navigates this new world, guiding readers towards clarity, purpose, and intention. Ryan personifies authenticity, leveraging his personal journey and expertise in personal growth, wellness, and entrepreneurship.

He believes you should live according to your values, despite what the world may think. I couldn't agree more.

Amid the overwhelming demands for our attention, *Listen* beckons us to turn inward, focus on our own narratives, and chart a course that resonates with our true selves. As you delve into this book, I encourage you to immerse yourself fully, reflect on its wisdom, and rekindle a relationship with your core values and hidden skills and talents.

Kudos to Ryan Fahey for crafting this irreplaceable guide to self-realization in a distraction-riddled world. As you tune out the world and tune into the pages of this book, may it serve as a lighthouse, steering you towards a more genuine, grounded way for being, working, and playing.

- Brandi Heather

CEO, Speaker, Best-Selling Author,

Restoring, Retaining and Re-engaging Our Caring Workforce

September 5, 2023

INTRODUCTION

Who are you becoming, really?

When was the last time someone asked you this question? Probably never, because we don't have space to either ask or answer questions like this due to the busyness of our lives and the noise that creeps in day to day via email, social media, and phone calls, to name a few. From jam-packed schedules to endless meetings, calls, and notifications, it's no wonder we can't seem to handle answering the one question that really matters most. In a world moving faster than ever, we need to take a moment to really think about this question, which is why I wrote this book and why I am glad you have chosen to read it.

Your life doesn't transpire in a vacuum. Rather, it ebbs and flows like water, gushing or trickling from here to there, yet somehow moving with purpose, order, cause, and harmony. So what happens when you feel like life is flashing by, sucking you up instead of pulling you to shore? When you are too exhausted to swim with the tide? You become entangled, confused, distraught, and lonely. This is where many find themselves today.

Many of us turn to substances, vices, and expensive societal status symbols to fill this void rather than simply listening in and allowing our hearts to guide us as we journey through this thing called life.

Growing up, I always thought that life was very interesting on so many levels.

Some locals from my home community might even argue that I was one of the most reflective, introspective kids they knew. I constantly asked elders and other adults how they knew that "XX" decision was right and how they were able to make this thing called life work so well for them. Although the answers I got in return were always mixed, and sometimes perplexingly simple, no answer was ever the same. And yet, they all shared a commonality: I found that each person I asked followed the same pattern of listening to where life was taking them, and answering from there. This, I thought, was just so impressive. How does one acquire the wisdom to listen to one's life and to know how and when to act? How does one trust their heart enough to let it guide them? Where are the contracts? What about that exceedingly large salary? What about investing and making millions? What about becoming a YouTube star or TikTok influencer? How can we achieve prosperity if we are just sitting around and listening to our lives?

As I approach my fourth decade on this beautiful planet, I feel an increasing need to dive deeper into the idea of listening to your inner self; to where your life is taking you - especially in a world where we can be anything or anyone at any time. This is the same world that promotes communication over connection, clickbait over self-reflection; the same world largely void of purpose or cause, filled with demands to move fast, pivot now, and grind it out at all times. I wanted to write a book that prompts you to do the opposite: to turn *off* the noise and turn *on y*our heart and mind to what is actually happening to and around you, regardless of what chapter of life you find yourself in or what the noise around you screams for you to do or be.

One can argue that once we tune out our hearts, we have lost ourselves and the core of who we are. This drainage of self is an epidemic in and of itself as we seek to live an Instagram-worthy life over a life lived well. Instead, your life should ebb and flow from one deep desire and passion to the next while remaining fully aligned and harmoniously values-driven along the way. Water doesn't change direction without some force - it just is. What makes millions of people around the globe flock to oceans is arguably the solace that comes from the sound of wave after wave approaching and receding the shore in a repeatable pattern. It soothes us, relaxes us, and fills our souls. Your life should be the same. It should follow the consistent flow pattern you desire through the force you create.

Listen: How To Be You in a World Where You Can Be Anything is designed to challenge your thinking and create space in the margins of your life for you to better listen, and understand who you are becoming and what is really happening in your life. I wrote this book to take you on a personal alignment journey, and also to provide you with the space to start making your life what it is truly meant to be: a life lived at the highest levels of fulfillment, soaked in harmony. The ideas, concepts, and strategies outlined in this book are both game-changing and soul-filling. Embrace them and let them rush into your soul like the most beautiful wave you've ever seen.

Turn off your notifications and tune in to the pages of this book. Stop doing and start being. You have the rest of your life to answer that email. Right now, truly listen.

Lean in.

Your heart, soul, and future self deserve it.

Chapter 1:

THE AGE OF FLUIDITY

Modern times reveal modern challenges and one of the greatest challenges in our time is going to be deciding who we want to be in a world that tells us we can be anything or anyone. Being authentically oneself in the age of fluidity is the ultimate goal.

Fifty years ago, life was pretty standard for most folks. Go to school, get a job, buy a house, raise kids, retire after thirty years of working for the same company, and ride off into the sunset with a golden handshake. Paths were well charted early and most people didn't experience drastic job-related shifts over the course of their career.

It was also a period when humanity embraced some of the fastest technological advances of all time, including space travel and moving from the radio to the television. This was also the time when we started to see more women enter the workforce, which led to the rise of convenience foods such as TV dinners and an increased use of drive-thrus across North America.[1] Technological advances accelerated our ability to decide less so we could decide more and it accelerated the ability to have more disruption and more options for our lives. Why? Because as technology improves so does efficiency, and when efficiency improves it makes space for greater profits and innovation in the form of divergent products. Cereal is a great example of this. First, we had corn flakes. Then, we added sugar to them, creating Frosted Flakes. Then, we condensed it and put boxed cereal into what we now know to be the cereal bar.[2] Two choices became three. Three suddenly become a dozen. Restaurant menus grew larger, and the decision tree in pretty much every area of modern North American life expanded at an exponential rate. Suffice it to say, this was the start of an age of choice overload.

Rapidly advancing technology not only sped up the options in front of us, but also led to our lives moving faster than any other time in human history. We began using the microwave to cook food faster, buying two cars over one so we could drive more, and, by the 1980s, we were exploring computer technology and new industries never seen before such as call centers, cable services, and others.

Fast forward to just ten years ago, we now have a phone that not only fits in our pocket but does more than any computer from the 1990s could ever dream of. We now have app software that detects what we want to buy, and when, creating the least amount of friction we've ever seen. Children are growing up knowing what an iPhone is before they can even read and, from an early age, are interacting within internet spaces more than in their local communities. Heck, we even have apps for finding friends virtually, negating the need to leave our couch to find them.

If you were to walk down the street today and ask ten grade seven students what they want to do when they leave school, odds are they will tell you they want to be a famous gamer or YouTube star, maybe even a TikTok or (insert the latest trendy application) influencer. Their future selves are being dictated *to* them from a very young age, rather than through mindfully thinking about who they really want to become and seeking out life experiences and wisdom from folks in their communities and leaning into school. There is no space for the latter when the world is constantly entertaining you and monopolizing your attention from the moment you start eating solid food.

While some may argue that this is a fascinating time, it may also be the most concerning time in recent history. Why? Because in a world where we can be anything and do anything, our downfall may be a result of decision fatigue, a lack of purpose and clarity, and, if we're not careful, a complete erosion of values while we attach our identity only to what we do, not who we are.

Although I have limited formal education around human nature, the market, and economics, I do understand some basic fundamentals. One of which is that you need to have people working in an economy for it to be a healthy one. I also know that humans, when left to their own devices, will choose the path of least resistance. If noble professions like teaching and nursing are no longer attractive or easy enough for the next generation of workers, we now have an added challenge that needs to be addressed: the erosion of these noble professions which are the backbone of society.

Though this erosion in societal values could be an entire book in itself, for now, let's discuss where we are and the shared realities of today's world that you and I are navigating. I began this chapter by theorizing that one of the greatest challenges of our time is going to be navigating who we want to be and what we want to do, when we could be and could do anything. An abundance of choice can lead to choice paralysis or even choosing not to choose. That becomes the path of least resistance. Easy decisions make us lazy. It can also lead to making more impulsive decisions based on current trends or what the influencers in front of us tell us to pursue. It can even lead to depression and an erosion of values and self-identity. While this is all deeply concerning, it is an unfortunate byproduct of today's age: the age of fluidity.

As someone who has intimately studied personal growth and development for over fifteen years, I am a big believer in not remaining static in terms of our identities and the stories we tell ourselves. I believe we can and should change. I believe that we should not be defined by what we did twenty years ago if we've put in the work to change ourselves and improve the lives of others. Growth is both necessary and good.

However, there is a big difference between growth and development from a place of values, self-awareness, careful reflection, and understanding and simply moving from one trendy topic or job to the next without a core foundation of who we are as an individual and what we value along the way. This is the biggest challenge that needs to be talked about around the dinner table today. We must start asking questions about who we want to become and what we value versus what we are doing or are going to do with our lives. We need to carve out space for experiences which create the necessary conditions to explore ourselves and to understand what we like and don't like at a deep, heartfelt level. Simply put, sometimes you need to slow down now to move fast later. Slow makes space for grounding – and grounding is good.

Now, why is this so important, and how does this connect with the greater topic of this book? Well, listening to where your life is taking you can only happen if provided the space, energy, and time to actually listen. Listening to your life doesn't happen through an app or through one influencer's viral message. It starts with you and defining who you want to become and what you value before turning yourself loose to live at your greatest potential, fully aligned with your values. Moving in the direction your life takes you involves a great degree of self-awareness, self-reflection, professional awareness, and being intimate with your soul, none of which can be achieved quickly or easily.

However, picking up this book is your starting point and these chapters are your toolbox for what happens next in *your* life.

Use these pages to slow down, lean in, and listen to where your life is taking you, regardless of how chaotic things may be in your current daily life. Take your pulse, listen to your heart, and focus on the environment and smells around you. Be present with yourself and let clarity you find flow into your soul. Use this book as a tool to combat distraction and as a way to come back to your center.

In the next chapter, I will unpack the bottomless economy we find ourselves in and how connecting with ourselves can allow us to use patience over speed when it comes to choosing what vocation comes next. The next chapter will propel you forward as you continue leaning in to who you were meant to be and unlocking the best version of yourself.

Chapter 2

THE BOTTOMLESS ECONOMY

Ambitions change but the act of being ambitious should not.

Alongside the age of fluidity, we also find ourselves at another very interesting point in time. Following an aggressive baby population boom after WWII, we are now experiencing a global population decline in many parts of the world, running in parallel to an aging population.

In Canada, between 2016 and 2021, the number of people aged eighty-five and older grew by twelve percent, which is more than twice as high as the growth of the overall Canadian population.[1] We also know that in the not-so-distant future, fifty percent of Canadians will be over the age of fifty.[2] Once we hit this average age, there is a strong possibility that the average age of Canadians never dips below fifty again, unless something drastic changes.

Despite these challenges, there are also opportunities. One of those being an essentially bottomless economy. A time where you can choose any job rather than a limited number of jobs choosing you.

When the majority of a workforce is close to or seeking retirement, there are an abundance of jobs that need to be filled but fewer folks to step into those roles. While this seems rather obvious, the interesting point I want to dive into here is the fact that along with being able to be anything and do anything you really want to do in the age of fluidity, it's even more important to remind yourself that there is really no wrong choice when it comes to doing a job or taking on a career path. *It is a decision, not a death sentence.* If your career or job doesn't work out, you can always switch and pursue something new. Fortunately, the next thirty to forty years may be the easiest time in human history to make those switches with the least amount of ramifications.

With the right training and dedication to a particular craft, anything is possible. In other words, a bottomless economy is an economy that has more than enough jobs for everyone - with space for creativity and innovation across multiple industries. As technology continues to advance, new problems can be solved. Why can't you be the one to solve them? As industries change, there are many ways to earn an income or, in some cases, eat for free. At the time of writing this book, Subway announced that if you changed your name to be "Subway [last name]" you will receive free Subway sandwiches for life plus $750 to cover the legal fees associated with changing your name.[3] While this is only limited to a few folks in the US now, in a bottomless economy ideas like this will grow and spread, creating more opportunities for you and I to eat for free too.

The rise in crypto gaming is another example. With endless play-to-earn games popping up in the market, folks can now play video games from home and earn a modest, part-time income. Check out the book *Gonzo Capitalism* by Chris Guilibeau for more context around this and many more examples of how the new economy is being reshaped before our eyes.

***

Below are some statistics that really put the bottomless economy into perspective in Canada:

40% of Canadian farmers will retire by 2030 and 66% of current Canadian farmers don't have a succession plan in place.[4]

Between 2016 and 2021 more than 1.4 million Canadians were aged 55 and older.[5]

By 2030, over 50% of Canadians will be above the age of 50, and the US is following a similar trajectory (as of 2014, 34% of the US population was aged 50 or older).[6,7]

As of July 2022, only 15.6% of the Canadian population was between the ages of 0 and 14. For comparison, in India, the same age group represented 25.7% of the population as of 2021, 10% higher than Canada.[8,9]

This means that Canada's labor force will grow slower than that of India's (if we compare work outputs per person). It also means that there will be less Canadians to fill future job positions, which will become available as the current labor force ages into retirement. Simply put, you can be anything in the next ten to twenty years and be employed doing it. Still don't believe me? Take a look at this demographic data from TD bank:

If 2022 was any indication, we might be starting to see the pace of retirements accelerate. The Labour Force Survey estimates that 266 thousand people retired in the prior 12 months as of December, representing a 17% increase over the prior two years.

We believe this trend is likely to continue. By 2025, we expect to see the number of people 65 and older grow by 1 million. Based on current participation rates, that means nearly 900 thousand workers will leave their jobs in the next three years... That is a 50% increase in the average number of retirees each year compared to the average of the last 10 years.[10]

But that's not all... Since COVID-19 ravaged and disrupted economies across the world, the influx and popularity of remote work has grown exponentially. At the time of writing this book we have slowly emerged from the pandemic and are part of the reconstruction of the post-pandemic economy. In this economy, downtown core foot traffic in major cities is stabilizing at half of its pre-pandemic volume, and office occupancy rates in cities like Toronto are still down almost twenty percent. Canadian workers are stretching out to smaller cities across Canada for space and a better work-life balance, choosing a morning kayak on the Atlantic ocean before Zoom calls rather than a commute to the office in bumper-to-bumper traffic.[11]

While this phenomenon presents its own set of challenges, it also presents a slew of opportunities if you just listen to where your life is taking you. For example, it's much easier to listen when you have room to breathe, feel restored, and have space to think. For me, this looks like sitting in the back yard with a hot cup of coffee or walking the trails around our house. Yes, I too opted for the small city migration in the work-from-anywhere, post-pandemic economy.

Which leads me to my final point for this chapter. *In a bottomless economy, you can work where you want to live rather than be forced to live where you work.* If you want to jump on your bike at lunch for a quick thirty minute ride, why not? If you can begin your work day a little earlier so you can end work earlier to make time for entertaining friends, why not? In a bottomless economy, you should feel empowered to make your work work for you and not the other way around.

I recently listened to a great *Fearless Future* podcast episode where Jeff Dolan, CEO of Wavve, unpacks the nuances of the push-and-pull that's starting to be felt in our bottomless economy from an employers perspective.[12] Hear his take by checking out the episode yourself using the link or QR code provided below.

https://tinyurl.com/fearlessfuture1

Here is an excerpt in case you want to come back and listen to this at a later date:

The world has changed so much. So there is a high percentage of micro-businesses that have been created over the last couple of years, and although people continue to work in their full-time jobs, they're still able to find ways to create these other forms of revenue or an outlet for their purpose or passion.

It also goes without saying that in a bottomless economy, you should test, prototype, and try different jobs and interest areas. Long-gone are the days where you do the same job for thirty years because that's all that's available to you. As we glimpse into the future, you will have an abundance of choice when it comes to your career, hobbies, and pursuits. It's important to take calculated risks and to pursue your choices with full commitment, drive, and passion. The bottomless economy, when paired with longer life expectancy due to advances in technology and medicine, presents the unique opportunity, which wouldn't have been imaginable just one hundred years ago, to pursue multiple careers within a career lifespan. For example, what if you were a real estate agent for ten years and then you decided to become a teacher for ten years?

Later in your life, maybe you decide to open an art studio for another ten to fifteen years. You can be more nimble than ever in the future economy, which is why books like this one are vital to guide your decision-making and thought processes along the way.

At the end of the day, the economy will become bottomless (at least in Canada) for quite some time. Since you are reading this book, you are in the driver's seat to test, pilot, and change who you are, what you do, and where you do it. The trick is to really listen, to your life and to yourself, so that the choices you make help you grow into and become the best version of you.

In the next chapter, I am going to unpack how to gain perspective and professional awareness and how to build wealth as you listen to where your life is taking you.

Chapter 3

PROFESSIONAL AWARENESS AND BUILDING WEALTH

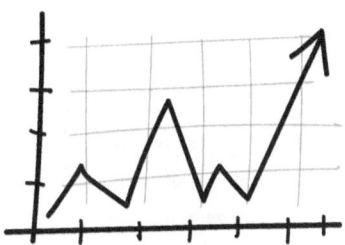

"If you have a dream, never stop preparing for that."
- Kurt Warner

There is a famous final scene in the iconic movie *Inception* where the main character, Cobb, spins his little tractricoid top and, after spinning for a few seconds, it is left barely standing as the camera suddenly cuts and the movie ends. As a viewer, you are left wondering whether or not the whole film was a dream. It is that final scene which makes you question what you just witnessed over the past couple of hours of film.

Our lives often mirror this end scene in many ways. We move cities, jobs, and even careers in a more fluid fashion than generations before. But are we consciously aware of the movements we are making? Are we professionally aware of each situation, opportunity, and force that is driving us from one move to the next? Are we consciously aware or simply dreaming?

Having professional awareness in the age of fluidity, within a bottomless economy, is a game changer. You must understand that in order to listen to where your life is taking you, you cannot gloss over this element and simply move from one thing to the next without order, consistency, purpose, and morality. If you do, you will find yourself looking back with regret, or becoming the topic of conversation at many dinner tables - for all the wrong reasons. ***Having professional awareness means knowing when it's time to go and when it's time to stay and grow.*** You cannot expect results overnight. Careers, as well as your legacy, take time to construct and art can't be rushed.

In my book, *Your Best Decade*, a concept I refer to often is the idea that your legacy is greater than your resume; that you shouldn't leave positions in shambles and bulldoze your way from job to job without consciously thinking about the legacy you are leaving behind. This is foundational to drive your professional awareness as you continue being you and listening to where life is taking you. For example, if you are simply moving from one job to another because you aren't happy (and the world tells us that we should be happy all the time!), what happens when you leave one job only to find yourself even less happy in the next? Or, what happens when you decide to take that promotion within your current job because the pay raise is great (and the world tells us that we should be making more money!), only to find out later that taking the promotion means giving up your evenings and weekends for the job? It is important to remember early and often that a rise in pay usually correlates with a rise in expectations. My rule of thumb is this: if your salary is six digits, be prepared to give more of yourself to that job. If it's under six digits, work hard but preserve those fringe hours and days for you and the things you value most outside of your work. Quality of life sacrifices just aren't worth the squeeze if your salary is under six digits.

In his book *Balance: How to Invest and Spend For Happiness, Health, and Wealth*, Andrew Hallam shares some research from Purdue University which supports this idea as well. According to one study with over 1.7 million participants, those who earned $105,000 per year reported higher levels, on average, of life satisfaction. Conversely, those who earned $60,000 had a lower level of life satisfaction.

Alternatively, those who reported earning more than $160,000 per year also reported having lower levels of happiness.[1,2] The point is, more money doesn't always equal greater happiness in life.

These are just some of the blunt realities you need to face head-on when listening to where your life is taking you. For instance, when considering a promotion, if you only look at what's on paper or what the number may be without considering what you may have to give up in order to make this added money, you may be setting yourself up for failure. It is important to ask yourself whether the promotion will compromise your core values such as family, fitness, or being a present parent. **What you turn down says just as much about you as what you pursue.**

Using professional awareness in this situation allows you to step outside of yourself for a moment to really think about all of the implications of a promotion, including how it could change your life – for better or for worse. On the other hand, using professional awareness isn't going to TikTok or X threads to get the "best advice" from "experts" who have been where you are. There exists no magic eight ball capable of giving you the answers necessary to make your decision on whether or not you take the promotion. Your circumstances, situation, values, and skill sets are unique to you. Others may have walked in similar shoes at similar times but ultimately you need to trust yourself and your own awareness of the situation before making a decision. Tough to do, I know, but trust me, journaling will help (*more on that later*)!

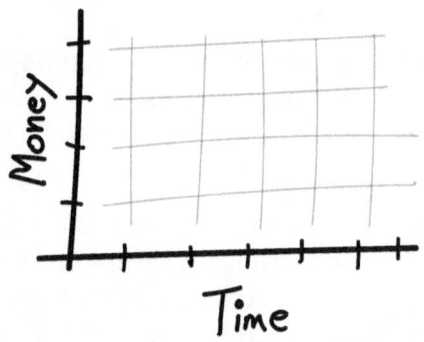

Building Wealth

We live in a time of exponential rising costs. From housing to food, the price of everything is rising quicker than we've seen in decades. Millions of us are experiencing this reality for the first time and the retirement horizon seems to be stretching further and further out of view. While it's important to build financial wealth and cover the costs of living, there is good news around generating wealth as long as you are willing to look at things differently.

In *The Everyday Hero Manifesto*, author Robin Sharma outlines eight forms of wealth we should be thinking about as we navigate life. Sharma's approach not only considers *prosperity* but also *adventure, impact, health*, and *family*, to name a few. In a society that values money over everything (capitalism at its finest!), it's a breath of fresh air to be able to look for and actively contribute to building variations of wealth across different areas of our lives.

I have taken Sharma's approach to wealth building in my own life, which has led to feeling more fulfilled, content, and in alignment with my core values. This is because his method taught me to focus on building multiple forms of wealth versus one singular form (i.e., money and assets).

Turns out, I'm not the only one to make this shift. According to the 2023 Charles Schwab Modern Health Survey, which surveyed 1,000 Americans between the ages of 21 and 75, "Non-financial assets like good health, fulfilling relationships and career flexibility resonate far more when defining wealth than having large sums of money." More specifically, a higher percentage of survey respondents indicated that well-being (40%) was a more important indicator of wealth than either money (32%) or assets (26%).[3] Wild and true! I hope we continue this trend moving forward.

> *For more on the eight forms of wealth, check out Sharma's book, or any of the additional career, life, and wealth building book recommendations provided at the end of this book.*

At the end of the day, in a world where you can be anything and accumulate a massive amount of wealth, it's important to stay attuned to the many forms of wealth, putting all forms on an equal playing field with traditional forms like money and assets. ***Re thinking your wealth is ok.*** Journal about how you are building wealth – with respect to your craft, your health and well-being and your family. It ain't just about the money honey! When you have enough to cover your needs, it's important to then measure your success and wealth in different ways.

In the next chapter, we are going to take a real look at what it means to be truly happy as you continue to block out the noise and become the greatest version of you in a world where you can be anything.

Chapter 4

HAPPINESS

"There is no way to happiness - happiness is the way."
— Thich Nhat Hahn

I'll be happy when…
You deserve to be happy!
You do you! (And then you will be happy.) Your happiness is the most important thing.

I've heard them all…

Happiness is one of the most clickbaited, marketable, studied, yet elusive words I have come across as an author, wellness coach, and speaker. As of 2017, there were over 23,000 books on the market with the word 'happiness' in the title.[1] According to Google Trends, searches for the word 'happiness' rose steadily between 2004 and

2020 (see image below), and yet a University of Chicago study revealed that only 14% of Americans said they were actually happy in 2020.[2]

Note: Google Trends was used to generate this data and accompanying image.

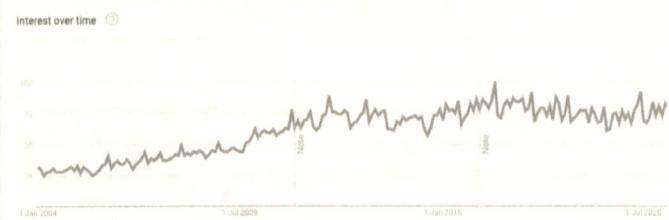

So why is it that so many folks are unhappy? Why is 'happiness' one of the most searched, most written about words but also one of the hardest states to achieve and maintain? The answer is simple, though not discussed enough: ***happiness is difficult to achieve and attain because happiness is fleeting***. Think about this for one moment. When was the last time you were truly happy?

What did it feel like? What did it sound like?

What smells do you associate with the experience?

Now, imagine a hornet enters the scene and stings you on the arm. Still happy in that same scene?

Probably not.

Capturing the feeling of happiness is like trapping a lightning bug in a bottle. Good for a moment but it won't last forever.

In my view, many of us are looking at happiness all wrong. We've tried to put it in a box and make as much money off of it as possible by making it as "achievably elusive" as possible. There is no market for happiness books if all their potential readers become happy.

This is why I argue that just as we need to look at wealth differently, we need to do the same when it comes to happiness. Viewing happiness as a continuum that can move across a spectrum rather than a feeling that we may or may not be able to achieve and attain as an end point is a great place to start.

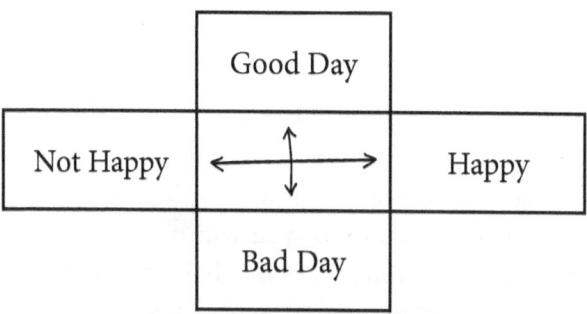

In reconceptualizing happiness as a continuum, it becomes obvious that happiness is indeed fleeting, and that at various points throughout your day you may be at various quadrants on the matrix. As you move from one quadrant to the next, it's important for you to dive deeper. You must go beyond thinking about the feeling of happiness to explore the hidden valley below. You must drill deeper. It's beneath the surface where you will find purpose, hope, healthy relationships, and fulfillment.

Circling back to Sharma's eight forms of wealth from *The Everyday Hero Manifesto*: this beautiful frame work helps describe how you might increase your overall happiness in life by reframing how you define wealth. The eight components of this model are as follows:

- Self-Mastery
- Health

- Family
- Craft
- Prosperity
- Mentors
- Adventure
- Impact

As I see it, these eight components not only make up our wealth but also your overall happiness (*more on wealth in the next chapter*). If you are excelling in your craft, investing in healthy family relationships, and mastering your own emotions, you will find happiness and success. The more you focus on enhancing these core life elements, the happier you become. This is why some of the most impactful leaders in human history had a sense of happiness that others couldn't imagine possible.

So, how do you seek out greater purpose, hope, healthy relationships, and fulfillment and how do you get granular on improving your happiness? In a world where you can be anything, how can you be happier within your own life?

Here's how:

Do a Values Audit or Check In

In my book, *Your Best Decade*, I emphasize how establishing and refining your values throughout life drives what you do each day and what you decide to put energy into. Getting clear on your top three to five values is the first and most important step to becoming truly happy each day. Why? Because once you have established or refined our top values, it's easier for you to make decisions on who you spend your time with, what you say "yes" to, and where you spend your energy and money. It allows you to trim out what doesn't align with your top values, which leads to harmonized living, and, in turn, joy, purpose and a deep sense of happiness, alignment, and fulfillment.

> For more strategies on establishing your core values, check out my best-selling book, *Your Best Decade*.

Create Your Personal Happiness Statement

Once your values are clearly defined, it's time to create your personal happiness statement. Let me be clear, this isn't an "I'll be happy when.." statement, but one that aligns with who you are as a person. Your personal happiness statement should be repeatable each day. Simply put, it's a present statement and not a future statement. It's a way of being today versus something you'll achieve later. What do you enjoy doing?

What fills you up? What brings you joy? These are good questions to ask yourself before creating your personal happiness statement.

Once you've created your personal happiness statement, write it down. Then review and refine it until you are one hundred percent happy with it (no pun intended).

Create a Personal Happiness Declaration (Commitment Device)

One of the core elements of behavior change and key to living in alignment with your values and happiness statement is an added form of accountability. James Clear, author of the NYT best-selling book *Atomic Habits*, refers to this accountability element as a "commitment device". He defines a commitment device as "any choice in the present that locks in future behavior".[3]

In my opinion, the best way to remain committed to both your values and happiness statement is by drafting and signing a personal declaration of commitment to keep you accountable day to day. To access my ready-to-use template, simply scan the QR code below or type this link into your browser:

https://bit.ly/3TTAA7k

Blueprint Your Perfect Day

In my best-selling book, *How to Thrive in Remote Working Environments*, I created a 5-Step Amplifier Blueprint(™) that remote and hybrid workers (and you as well) can use to help thrive in their craft each day. Building from that, when it comes to the pursuit of your personal happiness, it's important to first visualize what your perfect day looks like and then make it happen as often as possible. I know this sounds fluffy, but I can tell you from experience that this works. In positive psychology circles, this is referred to as *prompting* or *priming*.

Back in 2017, I had a big decision to make. Like with all big decisions in my life, I sought out more wisdom before making my move. I called a trusted friend and professional in life coaching who asked me this simple question: *"Ryan, what does your perfect day look like? Describe it to me."* So, as I drove down the highway, I began illustrating what my perfect day looked like. When I finished, she said, *"Now go make that happen. If decision XX leads to more of those days, go for it. If it doesn't, then maybe it's a pass"*. It was such profound yet simple advice that I hadn't really considered previously. She was right. I needed to visualize my perfect day, then figure out a way to make that happen as often as possible.

Since that conversation, I have consistently thought about my perfect day when making every big decision in my life. I'm happy to report that I've had many perfect days since that highway revelation, allowing me to enjoy life while living in harmony with my highest values - all because I sought out how to live by them as often as possible. I've spent the past seven years pursuing those perfect days and have had hundreds of them. I wish the same for you.

In your own life, it's important to ask yourself the same questions. What does your perfect day look like? What does it feel like? Smell like? Sound like? Visualize this, then write it down and make a commitment to yourself to make your perfect day happen as often as possible. Over my lifetime, I'm aiming to enjoy thousands of perfect days and it's entirely possible for you to do the same. Row in that direction and you'll be surprised what happens. Hint: *happiness*.

Replicate Your Perfect Day As Much As Possible

People have asked me many times, *"Ryan – what does wellness really mean to you?"*. My response is always the same: ***it's a series of intentional acts, done daily, which take you from living a good life to living your best life.*** Even more, it's about replicating your best days as often as possible. That, my friends, is a 56.6 billion dollar industry condensed into a nutshell.[4] Now get cracking!

What the industry often fails to do is equip us with what we need to live our best life. I believe this to be quite simple. You can't control the weather, traffic, or anyone else's mood but you can control whether you listen to what makes your best days your best and reflect on how to replicate those same conditions as often as possible. Think about it. ***If you have even 1,000 perfect days throughout your life, that's almost three years of life lived perfectly happily.*** I'll take that ticket please!

Follow the Breadcrumbs

In a world where you can become anything, if you are truly going to have a deep sense of joy, fulfillment, purpose, and happiness, it's imperative that you look for the breadcrumbs to guide you along the way. A journal can be a great tool to help you reflect back, find, and follow the breadcrumbs of success when you run into trouble or feel unhappy. I treat my journaling as a sacred space to record my highs, lows, moments of joy, and ambitions. Journaling leaves me feeling optimistic, deeply curious, and more stable in who I am becoming and where I want to be in my own life. This deep sense of fulfillment pours into everything I touch, such as my writing, conversations with my wife, and how I approach my craft.

If you aren't a journal person, I recommend reframing how you view journaling and restructuring your journaling process. Journaling can be as long or as short as you'd like it to be. Every entry is just that – an entry; it doesn't need to become a memoir. Journaling can also occur in different forms. For example, your journal could consist of a series of voice memos on your phone, a typed list of intentions, or a handwritten description of your day. Start small but journal often. Dedicating five minutes a day to journaling can change your entire life. Your journal will provide you breadcrumbs that reveal great things to you over time.

Plan a Quarterly Adventure

In 2021, things were quite chaotic in my life. I was in the trenches of my full-time job, on top of which I was running two businesses and managing one publication on Medium. My wife was in full-time school pursuing her Master's degree, while also continuing to work, and we were in and out of lockdowns more times than I could count.

This chaos was taxing on my mind, and negatively impacted my creativity, joy, and day-to-day energy.

To engineer our own escape, my wife and I planned a short adventure to Toronto for the holidays. On the train ride back to Ottawa, I wrote in my journal about how great this trip was for myself and for our marriage. It dawned on me then that I hadn't given myself permission since the onset of the pandemic to be the adventurous, curious traveler I had been in the past. All the fear and uncertainty perpetuated by the news had caused me to become a shadow of the traveler I once was. So, I created and wrote down a travel goal for 2022: Take a family adventure each quarter. Since then, my wife and I have lived by this and have gladly taken adventures every quarter. Some are further away and more extravagant. Others are close to home but still unique.

Whichever the type, these adventures have dramatically increased my happiness and improved our marriage. Setting this goal has also given me the space (and permission) to step away from my intense workload so that I can be more curious, adventurous, and joyful as a traveler to new areas. A quarterly adventure is something I recommend!

Seek Out a Swim Buddy

The Navy Seals have a swim buddy protocol during Hell Week. Essentially, your swim buddy's role is to prevent you from self-sabotage; to watch out for you during the intensive training period and beyond. Hell Week swim buddies typically form a bond that is so close, they remain watchful and connected for life. I believe that this phenomenon should not start and end within the Navy Seals. In our own lives, if we truly want to pursue the deeper parts of happiness, we need support along the way; we need someone who can call out our blind spots, help us course correct, and bring us back to reality. We also need a cheerleader, someone to lift us up when we need it most. A swim buddy can be just that: someone who will ask the right questions and nudge you in the right direction when it comes to listening to where your life is taking you.

Happiness doesn't happen alone – find your swim buddy and do life with them!

Seek Greater Impact

One of the most overlooked components to deep happiness is seeking out a greater impact in all areas of your life. Contributing to society and actively pursuing significant acts that improve humanity make us stand a little taller, sleep a little better, and breathe a little calmer.

Generating impact may come in the form of philanthropy, volunteering, or sitting on a local board. It could also come from taking in refugees, working to slow down the rate of climate change in your home community and country, or organizing a local fundraiser. No impact is too small or too large. It's about pursuing the greatest impact you can make given your current realities around time, money, energy, and influence.

The greater your impact, the more purpose you have and the more fulfillment you will experience. As you begin to see the effects of your impact through your leadership, giving, or ideas, the more you move beyond the surface level of happiness; the more you respond to the deep-rooted call of leaving a positive legacy, leaving this world a better place.

Be Proud of Your Craft

There is nothing better than finishing that final page of your manuscript, putting that last brick in place, or brushing that last stroke of paint on a masterful piece of art. If you truly want to be happy and live a rich, fulfilling life, you need to not only align your passion with your profession but also be proud of your craft and what you produce or accomplish through your work. Experiencing fulfillment and purpose within your vocation will leave you with a deep sense of pride in what you do, regardless of status, paycheck, or job title. Some of the happiest people I've ever met had no titles and few dollars to their name, but were so proud of their work. Work with purpose. In a world where you can be anything, if you aren't proud of what you do, who you are, or what you produce, it may be time to start questioning what needs to change for you to feel proud, fulfilled and alive with purpose.

As you tune in to your next move and continue becoming the best version of you, it's important to talk about timing in life. If you are truly going to listen and act without hesitation to where your life is taking you, you need to be conscious of your time and where you are spending it. In the next chapter, I will unpack this in detail.

Chapter 5

1 YEAR EARLY OR 1 MINUTE LATE

Fortune favors those who act early and often.

Many people say timing is everything and I couldn't agree more. There is one small problem with this statement though: it's too broad and at first glance doesn't have any real-life application. First, what does 'everything' mean? And second, timing means nothing if you wake up tomorrow with a stage four cancer diagnosis and only have weeks left to live. Universal statements and surface-level knowledge need to be reframed, especially when talking about listening to where your life is taking you in a world screaming at you to become something.

Along with "timing is everything", I've often come across the statement, "it's better to be one year early than one minute late". So, if timing is everything, and it's better to move earlier than later, I guess that means we'd better get a move on when it comes to figuring out who we are becoming and what we want to do with our time.

To use an example from my own life, back in 2017 I had a big decision to make. Do I stay at my current job, remain hopeful that things will change, and settle? Or, is it better to leave now while things are good, regardless of what the future holds? This would be a tough decision for anyone to make, let alone someone making that type of decision for the first time in their career. To put it plainly, I was terrified.

After reading some books, having multiple conversations with trusted mentors and friends, and reflecting on the decision and its future ramifications, I decided it was best to leave early. I have never looked back since.

Turns out, listening to how I was feeling and leaving that job early was an incredibly rewarding decision. Every time I run into old colleagues, it is almost always positive. We reminisce about the good old days and how we captured lightning in a bottle for a brief period of time (*more on that later*). There are no regrets or hurt feelings. Quite the opposite would have happened had I stuck around another year in complete agony. I would have been miserable and the first few years of positivity, cohesion, and connection would have been overshadowed by negativity and frustration, which is how people would have remembered me. Trusting my gut paid off and the same can be true for you.

What I thought was a risky, career-ending decision ended up being a catalyst for cementing life-long relationships and a decision that would propel me forward in the next chapter of my life.

In leaving a job or a season of life earlier than some career experts would advise, you can actually maintain solid relationships and celebrate the great moments along the way - for the rest of your life. Nothing can take away those experiences for you. No one can rob you of your good memories or fault you for doing what's best for you when operating at the top of your game. Sometimes it's ok to retire after the SuperBowl and to go out on top. Sometimes this is easier said than done – which is why I am glad you are still here reading this book.

In 2009, I remember my Dad picking me up at the local bus station and driving me home for a summer weekend. It was blistering hot; in fact, it was one of the hottest days on record that summer and my Dad was really stressed. He had worked for over twenty-five years in the forestry, conservation, and forest fire suppression industry and he was sure things needed to wind down. His stress that particular summer was high and expectations of him were even higher, despite the fact that he was being given increased responsibilities.

As the summer heat baked us in his truck that day, we talked about the timing of his retirement. He knew he could leave early (in two or three years) but also knew that if he stuck it out another few years, he could max out his pension, which meant more money during those golden years. After a lengthy discussion, I looked at his pale, stressed-out face and said, *"Dad, why stay? Why not go early and enjoy the years versus sticking it out for an extra two or three percent?"*. We hummed and hawed on that for a while. As that winter approached, my Dad made the decision to leave and announced his early retirement less than a year later.

A few years after retirement, while sitting around the campfire at our family cabin, Dad looked at me and said, *"You know Ryan, I am so glad you and your sister nudged me to retire early. I am so glad to have had less stress and my health over these past few years. It's been great."*. Now, my Dad is even more reflective than me, and when he speaks, he speaks with clarity, purpose, and cause. He was seriously grateful for the conversation which nudged him to exit early. My Dad retired a few years earlier than expected with great health rather than a minute too late with poor health as a result of excessive job-related stress. Well done Dad!

Truthfully, leaving early is really hard to both recognize and act on. Many captains prefer the nobility of going down with the ship over building their own life boat. While I am all for nobility, remaining resilient, and staying in the game when things get rough, I also believe that there is a fine line between persistence and stupidity when staring down the question, *"Is it time for me to move on?"*. Resilience and banging your head against the wall are two totally different things.

Here are five things to consider when staring down this question in your own life:

1. Protect the Downside

When building the courage to leave something (especially early) it's important that you protect the downside by playing out the decision in your head. Some good questions to ask are:

What will my life look like if I make this decision?

How will this decision impact others in my life?

What areas of my life will be most affected by this decision and how?

Are there any other ramifications to consider when making this decision?

What actions can I take now to prepare for the new reality that lies ahead?

Do I have at least three to six months' worth of savings in an emergency account to cover the time I may need for what comes next?

Answering these questions should give you confidence knowing you've thought through the decision in detail and are ready to act.

2. Will ≠ Change

Sticking around just because you think you can will things to change inside a company averse to change is a race towards fool's gold. This is also known as the sunk-cost fallacy: *"The phenomenon whereby a person is reluctant to abandon a strategy or course of action because they have invested heavily in it, even when it is clear that abandonment would be more beneficial."*[1]

As much as you may want things to change in life and in your career, change is traditionally slow and often dictated by decision-makers around you. Generally, those who have the gold (or power) make the rules and you often relinquish control when you sign up for a job and conform to the environment you find yourself in. There are times when you can will things into existence through sheer force, but positive change in a large, interconnected, hierarchical system is not easy or feasible for you to take on alone. Even in smaller groups and in close relationships, *change can be complex and have little to do with you and more to do with those involved in actually making the changes.* Asking yourself whether or not the juice (sticking around) is worth the squeeze (positive change in your favor) is an important one in deciding whether to stay or go. For more on this topic, check out Seth Godin's incredible book called *The Dip*, which dives deeper into identifying which career situation you may be in and what you should consider doing about it.

3. Opportunity Cost

Opportunity cost is paid when staying in your current situation (choosing to do nothing) leads you to miss out on other opportunities. Throughout the course of your life, you will outgrow things. Things like friendships, jobs, negative relationships, office culture, and college parties. Opportunity cost arises when you outgrow such things yet choose to stick around out of some twisted form of loyalty and nobility. When you do this, you lose out on other opportunities; opportunities to make new friends, land a better job, make more money, work from home, or build more fulfilling relationships. Case and point: if you went to university, how many high school friends do you still keep in touch with? Probably very few because you outgrew them when you pursued a higher education.

We are constantly changing and outgrowing things, sometimes at a faster rate than we are comfortable with. This lack of comfort is where the opportunities are waiting for you to grow, expand your network, and shatter new ceilings. Leaving early to pursue a more optimal opportunity (versus prolonging your current reality) is the most ideal situation for you to jump into. I encourage you to take the leap.

4. Willful Blindness

There are two other things that may cause you to stick around instead of becoming something different. First, you stay because it feels easier than leaving. Second, you stay because you convince yourself that things are not nearly as bad as they seem. While I am all about watering the grass on your side of the fence to make it greener, this thinking can lead to willful blindness. The danger of putting the blinders on is that they can mask how problematic the situation really is.

As Will Smith wrote in his recent book, *Will*, "reality always catches up to our dreams".[2] We can be dreaming of better each day but, eventually, we need to face reality. Avoid putting the blinders on and take a moment each day before watering the grass. If this doesn't prove to be enough, ask a friend or trusted mentor for their perspective. The famous Johari window framework points out that each of us has our own blind spots.[3] A trusted friend or mentor can be great at calling those out for you so you can avoid willful blindness. Simply put, have a trusted swim buddy.

5. Values Alignment

When discerning whether or not it is time to end one chapter and start a new one, it's important that you come back to your top three to five values and ask yourself whether or not your current situation (job, relationship or opportunity) still aligns with your top values. If not, it may be time to move on. An added bonus of using this approach is that when you make a decision based on your established values, no one can fault you for the decision you've made. Your values are unique to you and you know yourself best. **Others can judge all they want, but it really doesn't matter when you are moving in harmony with your core values.**

For a resource on establishing clear values, scan the QR code below or email me at faheyconsulting@gmail.com.

At the end of the day, in a world where you can become anything, toxicity, job complacency, depleted stores of willpower, willful blindness, and values friction can all clutter up the space you need to move forward clearly and confidently. Coming back to what you value most, speaking with a trusted friend or mentor, seeking out quality advice (*more on this later*), and doing some reflective thinking will help you better listen to where your life is taking you.

In the next chapter, I will talk about how to swim with the tide because, after all, listening is only half of the battle. You also have to know when to swim so you can effectively roll with the tide.

Chapter 6

SWIM WITH THE TIDE

It's wise to swim with the tide rather than against it.

In Barack Obama's book, *A Promised Land*, he recounts a conversation he had with Ted Kennedy when he was starting to rise in popularity with the American people. To make a long story short, it was Ted who nudged Barack to put his name in the hat for the President of the United States of America. Ted told Barack that sometimes you can't stop a rising tide.[1] He was right. Despite your own doubts and narratives, sometimes destiny comes calling. Momentum cannot be stopped and, as much as you want to swim against the tide, you just need to turn around and surf the wave all the way to the shoreline. As history tells us, Barack Obama went on to not only become the youngest President of the United States of America, but the first African American President, serving two healthy terms as the leader of the free world. Clearly, surfing the tide was not only inevitable, it was the right thing to do.

In listening to your own life, as Barack's story inspires, sometimes you need greater perspective. You need to get out of your own way and listen to those in your life who believe in you, despite your own limiting beliefs. This is hard to do in a world that screams at you to control your own destiny at all costs and to work until your hands bleed, until you have nothing left to give.

I am not suggesting you ride around doing nothing productive with your time to improve your life and the life of those you love. I am suggesting, however, that you sometimes need to be mindful and understand that you are on a specific trajectory, whether you like it or not, and that there are forces beyond your control influencing what happens next and how. In other words, you are not alone in shaping your destiny. It's your job to be ready to surf the wave when it's time.

In 2011, I was preparing to graduate with my undergraduate degree in Human Kinetics from St. Francis Xavier University. I watched as my peers applied to multiple graduate schools, hoping to get accepted into at least one. Some had a clear direction on where life was taking them and who they were becoming, but many were also looking around the room with imposter syndrome concerning the next step. Am I making the right choice? Did you hear what Sam is doing next? Did you hear that Dave got into med school? All around me, I could see a lack of trust in their own gifts, talents, and skills.

I remember thinking that my next step was a degree in education. I was passionate about sport, human movement, entrepreneurship, and education. I also knew that I wanted to spend the next few years in the town I was in to further develop relationships and build my side business of personal training. So, despite all the noise, the atmosphere of doubt, and numerous unanswered questions, I only applied to one graduate program: the education program at St. Francis Xavier University. I felt the tide was with me and that it wasn't yet time to leave the community that had nurtured my recent growth. I felt that I had more to give and that this school would allow me to do what I wanted, while also opening many doors.

I was shortlisted and brought in for an extensive admittance interview. I sat down with two other hopefuls across from the interview panel, which included the chair of the department As we took turns answering the panel's questions, I remember that about halfway through the interview, the chair looked directly at me with a cold stare and asked, *"Ryan, have you applied to any other programs?"* I answered, *"No"*. He countered by probing, *"Why not? What is your backup plan if you don't get into this program?"*. My response: *"If I'm not good enough to get into this program, I don't want to go anywhere else."*. *"Fair enough,"* he responded. It's been nearly twelve years since that interview and we remain connected today. And yes, I did get into the program. I trusted where my life was taking me and I swam with the tide.

To provide another example, in 2020 when COVID-19 hit, I remember pondering whether I should write my next book or not. A voice inside me just kept screaming to write it, telling me that it was inevitable that I would write something both timely and great. I hesitated, convincing myself that it was not the right time to write a book, an opinion shared by some others around me. However, once I accepted that I needed to listen to what my life was telling me as an author, I went from being on the sidelines with an idea to being unstoppable with a best-selling product. I wrote the manuscript in fourteen days and it became a best-seller within six months. Once I got out of my own way, I was able to get focused and trust my skills as an author. I was able to swim with the tide all the way to the top of the charts. Needless to say, the book changed my life and I am glad I listened.

These are just two snapshots to show you that swimming with the tide is not only a strong option on the table for you, but that it can also be life-altering. As you push forward, you expand your comfort zone, make new connections, deepen existing ones, and gain life experience along the way. You also develop an even deeper level of trust in yourself. These are extremely valuable assets to add to your knapsack and life resume as you continue becoming you and navigate new chapters of your life.

Mandela

Nelson Mandela has to be one of the most written-about leaders of all time. Many know his story of rising from the ashes of imprisonment on Robben Island to becoming one of the greatest leaders of our time. Though the system held him down for twenty-seven years, Mandela is a great example of fulfilling one's destiny and swimming with the tide. At any point during those twenty-seven years of imprisonment, he could have mailed it in, accepted his current reality, or abandoned himself altogether, but he didn't. He waited, he grew, his skin thickened, and when the tide eventually rolled in he surfed it in style.[2]

Swim With The Tide

Like Barack Obama and Nelson Mandela, we can find examples all around us of leaders who swim with the tide. We can find them in our current political systems, where the up-and-coming leader suddenly moves from being the opposition to being unstoppable. We can also find them in sport, especially in the world of Major League Baseball (MLB) during the month of October. Almost every year there is a MLB team that somehow rises at the right time, seizes their opportunity, and goes all the way to winning the World Series. It may not be the best team on paper, but when its players take the field, they become unstoppable *(more on this later)*. This is what makes sport, politics, and life so rich and interesting. At any moment, the tide can turn and the underdog suddenly becomes the champion.

In your own life, are you reaching that point where you are no longer just the opposition but are unstoppable? Are you the underdog that needs to get out of your own way by overthinking less and acting more so you can just keep winning? Do you already believe you can be all you were meant to be? Is there an inner voice that is telling you that it's your time? Maybe it's time to start pondering these questions as you continue becoming the best version of yourself in a world where you can be anything.

The tagline of this book says *Listen More. Do Less. Become Extraordinary.* That is my wish for you. Overreacting and overcompensating in the sport of swimming gets you nowhere. While consistently hitting your strokes and focusing on the simple things like your breathing can make all the difference between winning and losing. It's not about doing more, it's actually about doing less while moving through the water as efficiently as possible. That is the difference between average swimmers and extraordinary swimmers. Which are you?

In the next chapter, I will share why you should be cautious when seeking advice from folks you wouldn't trade places with. In a world where you can be anything, you can't become the best version of you by trotting with turkeys instead of soaring with eagles. In my experience, turkeys tend to say a lot without ever leaving the ground. On the other hand, eagles say very little and instead soar, wait, act, remain sharp, and observe carefully.

It's time to listen less to the former and more to the latter. Let's go!

Chapter 7

CAUTIOUSLY SEEKING ADVICE

Never take advice from someone you wouldn't trade places with. Period.

A big part of navigating this thing called life is taking advice along the way. I'm not talking about seeking advice on whether you should add a tomato to your sandwich. *I'm talking about asking for deep, life-altering wisdom when you need it most.* You may seek this type of advice during a time of vulnerability or a period of grief or loss. Or when you are on the highest mountain and on top of your game. Whatever the situation, scenario, or magnitude of the decision, you need to be cautious about who has your ear. This is why the President of the United States's Chief of Staff (arguably the most important position in the oval office) is appointed by the

President themself rather than elected by the people. The President knows who they need in their ear and knows how valuable it is to trust that person as the leader of the free world.

Proceed With Caution

A few years ago, an overweight person living with type 2 diabetes tried to give me unsolicited nutritional and fitness advice. Although the advice wasn't all that bad, I struggled to really take it in and apply it to my life because I just couldn't fully apply such advice from someone I wouldn't trade my health and fitness with. Lifestyle choices convey a sense of trust and reliability when sharing wisdom and advice with others. In other words, if you don't appear to be living by your own advice, why should I? Or, if your advice doesn't seem to be working for you, why assume it will work for me?

You can find prime examples of this peppered throughout the fitness industry. Look at the most successful trainers in the world. I guarantee they don't have a twenty-five plus body mass index or an unbalanced amount of body fat. Don't believe me? Google "the best personal trainers in the world" and look at the first five hits. What do they look like? I doubt any of them are out of shape or carrying much excess fat.

Another case and point: would you have done P90X back in the early 2000s if Tony Horton were overweight and out of shape? Likely not.

This phenomenon isn't unique to the fitness industry. In many fields, indirect marketing (i.e., how you look, what you wear, etc..) portrays a level of trust and reliability to prospective clients. As a professional in any field, how you present yourself matters. This is why most lawyers still wear suits and people stand up just a bit taller when a soldier walks past them in full gear. This is why many world leaders still wear a tie and why the late Queen Elizabeth carefully dressed for every event to match the tone in which she was appearing. This correlation directly translates to how you should seek advice and guidance throughout your life.

You see, when looking for advice, we tend to gravitate to people we would trade places with in an instant versus someone we just met on the street who looks tired, disheveled, and out of place. We're conditioned to embrace certain clothing color tones, facial gestures and postures. This is why many of the most successful Hallmark Christmas movie covers feature red and green color tones. We gravitate to those colors during the holiday season because we associate them with comfort, warmth, joyful memories, and nostalgia.

When listening to where your life is taking you, it's vital to be cautious about who you take advice from. You must treat all advice you receive with caution, absorbing and applying knowledge and wisdom to your life only from those you trust and respect the most. I believe that you become the sum of the five people closest to your ear and that to live at your fullest potential, you deserve the best you can get.

The next time you are offered unsolicited advice, ask yourself if you'd trade places with that person before applying it to your life. The answer to this question will tell you whether or not you should integrate that particular advice or wisdom into your own life.

So, what about taking advice from those we love most, even if we wouldn't trade places with them? Well, this presents a unique challenge. A good example is family. Take parents. We love them (I hope that's the case for you!), but just because we love them doesn't mean we would trade places with them. We may not wish to replicate some of their career and/or life choices. The same can be true for siblings and other relatives. If we are going to reach our full potential, we must acknowledge our need to seek advice and wisdom from those who have walked a similar path, experienced a similar struggle, or overcome a similarly difficult chapter of life. Don't let love get in the way of your self-worth. A plane cannot overcome excess drag or weight no matter how much love you put into it. It's just physics.

It's equally important to remember that just because you aren't taking advice from someone you love now due to the decision, action, or options in front of you, doesn't mean you won't in the future. Your life should be designed and lived in a way that allows you to activate different relationships for advice and wisdom channels depending on what you are looking for and where you are on your own life journey. For example, even in my own life, I seek advice from different people for different decisions. I also expect there to be friction and not a clear-cut answer or way forward. I absorb what I can, take in all perspectives, and then make the clearest and best decision possible for me.

An additional aspect of choosing who to seek advice from is how many people to consult. I recommend not seeking advice on something big with more than five people because doing so can lead to mass confusion and move you away from trusting your gut. Trust me, I've been there and it doesn't end well. When faced with a big decision in your life, only seek enough advice and wisdom to formulate your decision with clarity. Five people in your ear will do that. Seven people will lead to too many possible options, opinions, and outcomes, creating mass confusion, overstimulation, and decision-paralysis. *Stick to the rule of five and you will be set with a clear way forward.*

Now, there will be times when you need to do things your own way, despite what is being spoken into your ear by those you trust most. I define these moments as "intrinsic gut nudges", which are nudges that come from a place deep inside of you and which move beyond reason, rationale, and logic. Call it nature versus nurture, fight versus flight, intuition, it really doesn't matter. It's an internal barometer that doesn't give a damn about the cards on the table, the voices in your ear, or the pro-con list you wrote in your journal. Many entrepreneurs need to act based on intrinsic gut nudges or else miss out on life-changing opportunities. Many authors, for example, were likely rejected four or five times before their work ever got published. Even J.K. Rowling was rejected multiple times. I'm sure in those moments she had folks around her wondering when she should move on, but she followed her gut and now her books are internationally acclaimed.

When you truly listen to where life is taking you, you can't ignore the feeling of knowing you need to push forward. Yes, this is the point in the book where you realize that you may, in fact, have little control at times over where your life is taking you and you need to be ok with that. *Your life is an unfolding story not a puzzle to be solved.* Sometimes, life requires you to be alone with your thoughts versus acting on what your thoughts are telling you. Life also requires the opposite, via inaction or aggressive action. Taking action may involve reshuffling what's been dealt on the table or it may involve you flipping the table over altogether. Despite any advice or wisdom shared with you, only you can act, pivot, or move on. What will you do?

Unmet Expectations

If you are afraid of what others may think of your decision or way forward after taking (or not taking) their advice, don't be. Expectations are often emotional fabrications that bind us to who we are now, holding us back from our future self. The hard truth is that many speak and few act. You are a person of action and no one can be upset with you for taking action in your life to move forward in your own way.

A Final Piece of Advice

Now, before we move on to the next chapter, focused on preparation and self trust, I want to return to the opening sentence of this chapter. Please, please, please, do yourself a favor. In a world where you can be anything and as you seek to listen to where your life is taking you, don't take advice or seek wisdom from someone you wouldn't trade places with. Even when you love them.

Life calls you up, not down.

Ascend.

Chapter 8

TRUST AND PREPARATION

Something beautiful happens when trust and preparation meet.

Nothing is more frustrating than preparing like the harshest winter is ahead yet having a lack of trust in yourself and your ability to weather the season. The same holds true when you trust yourself to do anything in the world but don't properly prepare. It's an unequal marriage that is set for disaster from the get-go.

However, the opposite can also be true. When trust and preparation meet, your life changes and the world around you gets put on notice as big things start to happen. Confidence breeds competence in a virtuous cycle. Infused with action, this is where you start living your life to the fullest. When trust and preparation meet, the world seems brighter, the opportunities become more abundant, and every downside has a silver lining because there is no challenge you can't overcome.

Trust

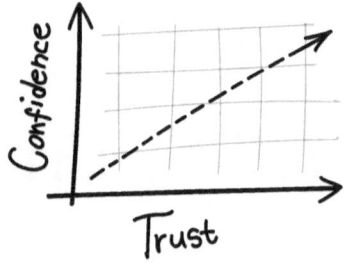

Preparation

In a world where you can be anything, marrying trust and preparation is absolutely key to achieving success in whatever you choose to do and who you become. There is no escaping the significance of the intersection between trust and preparation.

In 2023, I finally started to connect with speaker bureaus across Canada to become listed among their family of professional speakers. I trusted my decade-long speaking experience and the preparation process I used to successfully speak on over seventy-five podcasts, conferences, and events around the world. My experiences yielded a deep trust in myself and refining my preparation process over time allowed me to deliver high-quality speaking engagements. Many of these preparation hours go unseen, regardless of what you pursue, but remain necessary to experience greatness in your field.

Still don't believe me?

Let's take a look at Olympic sprinters. They train for years to run a single 100-meter race in under ten seconds. Trust and preparation meet on the starting blocks, as these athletes have practiced launching out of the blocks more times than they can count. They know exactly

Trust And Preparation

when to launch, when to hit top speed, and when to lean forward to edge out their competitors at the finish line. When you watch these 100 or 200-meter races at the Olympics, the process seems so routine to these athletes that they almost look too comfortable and relaxed after the race. All a result of trust meeting preparation.

In life, sometimes opportunities pass us by. Losses can stack up, which can prevent our confidence from growing and, in some cases, start to form as micro-traumas. If this has happened to you, I want you to remember that as your trust and preparation continue to collide in the future, good things will come to you – often when you least expect it. In the meantime, here are some tips to help you break the cycle of dwelling on a loss or regret and build inner trust for the next opportunity, relationship, or critical conversation.

1. Journaling

For the past ten years, I have been a huge proponent of journaling. It not only leaves you with breadcrumbs for building life-long success, it also contributes to your inner confidence and trust. For example, think back to the last big decision you made. How terrifying was it? Did you almost not make it? What would your life have been like had you not made the decision? Now, imagine having the answers to all of those questions readily accessible in your journal. Powerful stuff. Documenting decisions, milestones, and significant moments in your life will set you up for greater success as you continue to move in the direction your life is taking you. Think of your journal as your personal story being documented by you and only you. You are the blank canvas and each day, decision, or big moment is waiting to be recorded. Don't let this critical information and your unique stories fade into memory. Write them down. Build inner trust in your ability to execute and make big decisions. Repeat.

2. Reflective Thinking

Philosopher John Dewey first popularized what we now call "reflective thinking",[1] a true game changer. Teachers are some of the best reflective thinkers, as they are constantly scanning their notes to discover how they can deliver a better lesson plan and improve student learning. It's so focal to the profession that it typically ends up being built into the professional growth plans of millions of educators around the world each year. Why can't we have that same reflective rigor in our own lives? When we experience a loss, it's ok to reflect and work through how you would change or improve for the next go around. When we experience a win, we should do the same so that we repeat it; so we can excavate the ingredients needed to achieve success in the next chapter, moment, or opportunity. Reflection goes hand-in-hand with journaling, two practices that are foundational for building your inner trust. Build some time in your calendar this year to just be and reflect. Even business mogul Bill Gates is known for taking 'think weeks' each year to reflect and gain clarity away from the busyness of work and life.[2]

3. Become a Better Narrator

In *Your Best Decade*, I included an entire chapter on the stories we tell ourselves, a popular topic among many authors in the personal growth arena. At the end of the day, if you want trust and preparation to meet and produce huge results in your life, you first need to be mindful of the stories you tell yourself and, if necessary, start telling yourself new ones. Perfect example: when I was writing my last book, *How To Thrive In Remote Working Environments*, imposter syndrome kicked in big time. I didn't think I was worthy of writing a book about well-being for the global remote and hybrid workforce. However, through journaling, reflecting, and telling myself a new story, I wrote a book that went on to achieve great success and add value to the lives of thousands of people around the world. Trust and preparation need to be given a chance to work. Even if you prepare endlessly, if you keep telling yourself it's impossible and that you aren't enough, you won't go on to succeed. Excuses kill creative action. Shed that skin and evolve. Tell a better story that elevates and moves you forward. Life is too short to stay in the mental halls of a self-depreciating house.

4. Know Your Worth

Sometimes, trust and preparation are there, but the opportunity or big moment doesn't happen. Do you pack it in and go home? Absolutely not. Know your worth. Sometimes this means adding a zero. Let me explain.

A few years ago, I was rejected from two speaker bureaus and two speaking gigs because I either didn't charge enough for my speaking or didn't make enough as a business owner. These were some stark moments where I had to turn inward, reflect, and figure out how I was going to break through these walls. Everything was there with my business and with my speaking, yet things weren't adding up. I realized that I was undervaluing my knowledge, ability, and experience. So, I decided to add a zero to everything. From my speaking fees to my services, adding a zero was the best decision I ever made for my business.

Even though my value-add was the same, that decision landed me an exclusive spot on an even more prestigious speaking bureau and it allowed me to double my income with my business. It also increased my confidence as a business owner and pushed away clients who were not committed or invested. $50 clients are not $500 clients and $500 clients are not $5,000 clients. People stand up taller when you charge more. You stand taller when you charge more and stick to your worth. Everyone looks when a Corvette drives by. You have to book a time to have gold flakes on your pastry while sitting on the Arabian Gulf in Dubai but you don't have to book a time to eat a Tim Hortons donut in Sudbury, Ontario. Which experience is worth more?

If there is one thing to take away from this chapter as you strive to become what you want to become in a world where you can be anything, it's to not dismiss the role that preparation and trust play as drivers to your success. No industry, vocation, or world-class art is shaped without these pieces at the center. ***You must give to gain.*** Give yourself preparation time and gain inner trust over time. The most successful business owners in the world have a deep sense of self trust and years of preparation. They've given it their all. Athletes are the same. Build the runway of success brick by brick, year after year, and watch your life change.

In the next chapter, I will dive into the seasons of growth that will come and go in your life as you listen

Trust And Preparation

to where life is taking you. In becoming extraordinary, growth is inevitable. It's not all sunshine and rainbows. Just as a ripe harvest experiences seasons of unseen growth beforehand, you will experience much of the same.

Chapter 9

EMBRACING THE FALLOW SEASON

Embracing a season of fallow now avoids a lifetime of failure later.

I grew up in a small town famously known for being the Blueberry Capital of Canada. As the title implies, yes, it had lots of blueberries. Every August turned into a borderline version of The Hunger Games on the sides of mountains all across Cumberland County, Nova Scotia as the short harvest season took over.

Blueberry fields, like those of other crops grown all over the world, go through a fallow season. ***This is a season of unseen growth, preceded by a season of bloom, beauty, and harvest.*** In other words, fallow seasons, in agricultural terms, are seasons during which land is worked – through tilling and plowing – but not sowed.

Instead of planting new seeds, the land is left alone with the goal of replenishing valuable nutrients needed to grow healthy crops. Time then does its part. What makes this season so unique is that growth can't be seen with the naked eye. Growth is constant, you just need to investigate it with the right lens to actually see it.

Enduring the fallow season is not always easy. Farmers around the world hope and pray each day that the growth they seek actually happens down the road and that the right conditions are present to ensure the land is nourished well enough to foster great blooms following the fallow season. However, there exist many variables that can influence the outcome of a harvest. When you can't see growth as it occurs, it is more difficult to trust and observe without pivoting or switching gears.

Today we live in a world where positive results are expected with little time or effort. A recent survey of US college students noted that these students believed they should be making over 100,000USD in their first job.[1] While this is an admirable goal, a first-job salary at this number is not the reality right out of the gate in many professions. Instead, it takes years of hard work, dedication to craft, and commitment to passion to reach such desired numbers. Results don't happen overnight.

In our own lives, we must acknowledge that in order to become who we are meant to be, we must embrace a fallow season - regardless of its length. If you want to be a prolific writer, this could mean writing one thousand well-written articles before becoming a mega success. If you are a singer, it may take releasing two or three albums (and many years) before you really find success on any industry billboard. Regardless of what you choose to do, a fallow season is warranted. Because of this, why not plan for it rather than being forced into it? Longevity is the only game in town anyway.

Here is a quote from legendary entrepreneur coach Dan Sullivan on growth, which paints an accurate picture of what planning for a fallow season looks like:

"Your level of capability in the future depends upon your measurement of achievements in the past. You can't move forward and grow until you've acknowledged how far you've come and have properly measured your gains."[2]

In a world where you can be anything, you also need to stay in the game long enough to fully become who and what you wish to be. The world is full of one hit wonders plaguing every industry from music to finance to big tech. It's easy to enjoy short-term success – with almost anything, but very difficult to achieve long-lasting success. Enduring success requires time and nurturing deep seeds of growth. You will mess up, make mistakes, and feel discouraged along the way. You will want to quit, run and hide, and can forget that your goals aren't as far out of reach as you initially thought. When this happens, it's important not to forget this simple piece of ageless advice: *If it was easy, everyone would be doing it.* But you aren't just anyone, you are someone uniquely capable of doing amazing things. If nothing else I write in this book sticks, trust that!

Longer Seasons

Not all fallow seasons are the same. Some professions may require a longer fallow season than others, and some seasons of growth may continue longer than you wish. Stay committed, remember why you chose what you did, and stick with it to the bitter end. The results will come. Trust.

For example, back in January of 2021, I was experiencing a fallow season with regards to a particular project I was trying to get off the ground. I tilled and tilled and tilled, preparing space for the project to take root, just as farmers prepare their land for seed. For hours and hours, seven days a week, I tilled.

I kept tilling because I wasn't focused on the *results*. I focused on the *process* instead. (P >r).

I remained focused on the process throughout the entire month knowing that at some point, during some waking hour, I would hit a breakthrough with results. Like farmers, I trusted the preparation process and that my field would eventually grow into a beautiful canopy of blueberries. And you know what? It worked! After the fourth week of continuous tilling, after spending about fifty hours on a specific project which was in fallow, my crop was ready to be harvested.

I moved from:

(P > r) — **PROCESS being greater than results**
to
(p = R) — **process equalling greater RESULTS**

Beautiful!

One of the strategies I employed during this fallow season to help me track my progress was intentionally journaling. Each week, I made notes about the small wins I was making throughout the process (*I call these "process wins"*), which both helped me keep track of my growth and remain on track.

Writing a book is often experienced like a long season of unseen growth and struggle. I can't tell you how many times I've wanted to give up as a writer, even though I've experienced success and have had thousands of people around the world read my work. I've had the urge to fold and give up on my authorship journey many times, yet I am still here.

In author John Milton's case, it is speculated that he had to delay writing *Paradise Lost* due to the English Civil War. By the time he was able to finish writing it, he was totally blind; however, with the help of an amanuensis to get the work to the finish line, *Paradise Lost* was finally published.[3] I think it's safe to say that Milton experienced a very long fallow season with this particular project, but he never folded. Milton weathered the fallow season and went on to create one of the most read works of modern time. A great example of a long fallow season that paid off.

Artists, writers, and filmmakers may take years crafting the perfect story, plot line, or piece of art before releasing it to the world. Iconic work takes time. Magic needs space and it often takes many fallow seasons of masterful, unseen work for results to roll in.

Shorter Seasons

If you are blessed to have shorter fallow seasons throughout your life, congratulations! This is a remarkable thing and something to celebrate. Just remember to record the season's learnings in your journal for when the inevitable long winter sets in during your next career, chapter of growth, or interest change.

My encouragement is that you take the time you need to be comfortable being in a season of fallow. Be ok doing less while being patient with your growth journey. *Fallow does not equal failure.* Instead, being in the fallow season means you have a tremendous opportunity to grow; when untouched by external stresses, you can replenish and prepare yourself for future growth.

Focus on the process when engaged in your hobbies, activities, projects, and goals. Remain focused on your values and goals. Be 'OK' in the fallow season and embrace it as such. Put the work in day to day, week by week and eventually you will yield a crop rich with results and ripe for harvest.[4]

In the next chapter, I will talk about what it truly means to capture lightning in a bottle, as well as how to look for the lightning around the bottle, as you lean in to becoming the best version of you and listen to where life is taking you.

It's time to make sparks fly!

Chapter 10

LIGHTNING IN AND AROUND THE BOTTLE

When you stick around long enough and continue to add value, sparks fly.

Capturing "lightning in a bottle" is an expression I've been fascinated with for many years. Originally attributed to Benjamin Franklin, the phrase hints at a desire to capture something extraordinary or to achieve rare success.[1] As you navigate a world where you can be anything, I truly hope you find that magical thing that makes you feel alive, and that you pursue it admirably with purpose and grace. I hope that you become great in whatever you choose to do. I hope that you manifest your own lightning in a bottle.

Lightning In And Around The Bottle

When capturing lightning in a bottle, or in achieving rare success, you need to work from your "sweet spot". *Your sweet spot is the space where your passion(s) and profession(s) meet.* It's the space where purpose and fulfillment dance with prosperity and harmony. It's perfectly aligned in every way. It's moving beyond fallow and into full bloom.

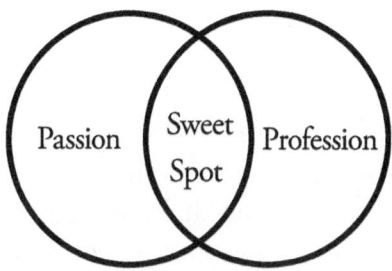

In baseball, this is known as the "October Effect". Or, when one team gets hot (i.e., finds its sweet spot) and goes all the way to the World Series. Here is an excerpt from MLB which sheds light on this phenomenon:

"Baseball in October is still baseball.... mostly. It retains the general properties of the sport of baseball, anyway. Regulation games remain nine innings, there are three outs per inning, four balls make a walk, etc. It's played in the same stadiums, with the same teams.

But if it doesn't look like regular-season baseball, that's because it's not. It's not a leisurely summer afternoon, one of 162 games over six months. Its baseball turned up to 11, then shot out of a helicopter, into the sun, with fireworks."[2]

When baseball is turned up to this level, it produces magic on ball diamonds across North America. Sparks fly late in the season and teams "get hot", fuelled by a real inferno that drives them deep into the playoffs, often to the World Series. On paper, the "October Effect" is really hard to explain because sometimes it involves a team with zero famous players, lower salaries, and an average standing in the league. In reality, it's a rare success being played out on the field from October to November. To help explain, here is a list of three teams that had no business making it to the World Series given their roster and early season statistics:

1. The 2000 New York Yankees

Summary – This was a relatively new and young team; the team was transitioning and not expected to win the playoffs. Sparks flew all season and on the backs of good pitching and solid hitting, this team won a legendary series against their rivals, the NY Mets. The team went on to crush records and make history for many years – all from a wild (and poetic) 2000 World Series win.

2. The 2006 St. Louis Cardinals

Summary – You can attribute this World Series win to Manager *Tony La Russa*. The guy is a legend and saw layers to the game the average person couldn't. He managed to win a World Series with a team which, in a good year for its division, wouldn't have made it into the wild card round of the playoffs.

Fun fact – I sat in the team's dugout in 2007 and still have gum from one of the players on my Red Sox jersey.

3. The 2010 San Francisco Giants

Summary – This team couldn't hit the broad side of

a barn during most of the 2010 regular season. However, come fall, the team's hitting improved just enough to make wins go its way. However, it was the pitching lineup that ultimately helped the Giants bring home the World Series championship that year.[3] It was so much fun to watch!

As you can see, statistics and names on paper don't tell the full story. They provide just one dimension. The other sides of the story come from what plays out on the field in another dimension influenced by situational awareness, motivation, focus, decision making, in-game management, team dynamics, confidence, and attrition. You can't draft this and you can't easily quantify this with a salary number – it's magic. At the time of writing this book, we are currently seeing this play out with coach Deion Sanders at Colorado University. The team won only one game last year and as of the start of the 2023 college football season, they are already 2-0, ranked as a top 20 college football team in the US, and selling out the stadium each week.

Many successful startups are connected to this concept as well. Startups often run lean operations where passion and dedication to the mission or product trumps ego. Teams can move fast, remain hyper-focused, and problem solve on the fly, all while supporting innovation along the way. Many entrepreneurs will say that the early days – before they became really successful – were special (and stressful) because the mission was greater than the sum of all egos involved.

In business, when you have the right people in the boat, rowing in the same direction, great things happen. Ego moves to the side, lightning strikes, and the team flourishes, becoming more than just a team. Each member joins together to become one harmonious movement. They become an unstoppable force. Ride that wave when you are on it. If you aren't on that wave, start looking for a team where you can be a part of it and seek ways to get on board. It's a magical thing to experience.

As you've already learned, in 2021 I became a best-selling author in Canada. The magic ingredients came together and, with perfect timing and execution, my book hit the market at the exact moment it was needed most. Was I better than other authors? Not necessarily. Was I first? Yes! Was I timely? Yes! Voila – the ingredients needed to achieve a rare success. It was timing, tactfulness, precision, and execution that manifested lightning in a bottle and turned my book into a bestseller.

Bottle = My book, an effort to support a global need (i.e., well-being for remote workers at the height of COVID lockdowns).

Lightning = Launching a high-quality book at the exact time the market needed it most.

Lightning Around The Bottle

In 2023, I wrote an article in *DataDrivenInvestor* on the importance of capturing lightning *around the bottle* as much as the lightning inside the bottle.

Here is an excerpt from that article:

As a best-selling author who coaches other aspiring authors to become successful, this is a focal point that I bake into my coaching program with clients from day one. Direct reads, audible streams, and book sales are only part of the equation.

The larger conversation is always the money that is around the book you are creating. Mastering that mindset and taking action early and often can allow authors to create their own form of rare success.

Simply put, lightning in a bottle is amazing, but finding the lightning around the bottle can be exponentially greater than what's in the bottle itself. Don't miss out on achieving a rare success because you weren't looking for it.

Take the early days of Airbnb as an example. In August of 2008, prior to the Democratic National Convention in Denver, Colorado, the minds behind the company relaunched their site, targeting that specific area and event knowing local hotels would be full. Airbnb accommodations hosted 600 people during that event. You could say that sparks were flying. CEO Brian Chesky and his team knew they had something special, and that was the beginning of Airbnb as we know it today. Was their product perfect? No. Was it filling a need for many people? Yes. The problem they encountered was trying to get folks to list their homes on their website, which required more marketing, more money, and a better website. So, they created their own cereal brand (lightning around the bottle) and used the sales ($30,000 worth) to help finance and scale Airbnb.[4] Brilliant!

Countless stories like that of Airbnb's creation have occurred throughout recent history. Facebook, Paypal, Strike, and Square are just some examples of how companies have manifested this concept and become successful. If you dig deep into any sphere, you will see this concept at play. Take Obama's rise to becoming President, Walt Disney's origin story, the global popularity of *Friends*, and Tesla to name a few. A commonality among these rare successes was the ability to harness lightning in a bottle without losing sight of the lightning around the bottle. Here's what I mean:

Barack Obama

Bottle: Charismatic leadership.

Lightning in the bottle: Stepping up for America at a moment of change.

Lightning around the bottle: "Yes we can" slogan, which motivated new voters to come out and a wave of change over two terms as President.

Walt Disney

Bottle: Mickey and Minnie Mouse characters.

Lightning in the bottle: Creating spin-off characters like Pluto, Goofy, Daffy Duck, and others.

Lightning around the bottle: Bringing characters to life by creating the happiest place on earth, also known as Walt Disney World.

Friends

Bottle: Sitcom about a group of friends all trying to navigate life in New York City.

Lightning in the bottle: No actor was a breakout star, making room for all actors to grow and mature on the show together, alongside their viewers.

Lightning around the bottle: Preserving the magic of the show by not adding another main character over the ten seasons and ending it on a high note, without spin-offs.

Tesla

Bottle: High-quality, high functioning electric vehicles.

Lightning in the bottle: Luxury electric vehicles – a new form of luxury at a time when the world is shifting to more green energy *(no need to compromise on luxury to go green)*.

Lightning around the bottle: Spin-off models at more affordable prices that don't compromise on luxury quality or the shift to green energy.

Apple iPhone

Bottle: Putting a computer in the palm of your hand.

Lightning in the bottle: Brilliant design, no more keypad buttons, customizability, moving away from older style cell phones.

Lightning around the bottle: Ability to accessorize with an iPad, Macbook, or headphones.

In a world where you can be anything, seek this. In your career, you may only experience this concept once. In life, it may be a series of chapters or it may be one particular moment, opportunity, or season which ends as a rare success. You may also have a full career of this as you transition from opportunity to opportunity. Whatever the case, don't take this rare moment for granted when it happens. Enjoy it, embrace it for what it is, and make it yours.

CONCLUSION

Just because you think you've made it doesn't mean it's time to take it easy. When everyone around you is throwing in the towel your resolve should be to bring it on.

As I conclude this book, I hope the concepts you encountered met you where you are at right now and gave you what you needed. In the next five or even ten years, I hope that you re-open this book and that the ideas within it hit you in more unique ways. *Books are timeless, and the best books are the ones containing messages that meet you where you're at when you need it most, time and time again.*

If this book left you in a better place, it would be a shame not to share that with others. If you can, I hope you will be ok with a genuine ask from me as an independent author before we part ways. If you head to Amazon and leave it a star rating (or a review) that would go a long way in helping this book reach others around the world. If you can tell either your neighbor or coworker about one thing you learned from the book, I'd love to hear about it on social media as well!

Leaving no stone unturned, as you become everything you are meant to be and carefully lean in to where your life is taking you, remember that greatness lives within. These pages were just a guide to show you how to embrace the greatness you already have within you. Everything you need to succeed and live a beautiful life is right in front of you, you just need to listen. One great way to do this daily is to journal. Journaling, as Matthew McCounaghey would say, helps you to *"get livin"*.

Life calls you up, not down. You are designed to become fully and uniquely you in your own way. Your words, actions, journal entries, and conversations matter. They can harmonize into something truly special in the form of your best self. You just have to do one thing: listen.

As you pursue your passions and vocations with deep obligation, remain true to who you are because at the end of the day, authenticity doesn't have a ceiling. Everything you are brightens the lives you touch, today and into the future. Don't be afraid to pivot, but be aware of the difference between getting out of the fight too early and sticking around to see how it all shakes out. Don't shy away from being a minute early in everything you do and remember these final words:

Listen more.
Do less.
Become extraordinary.

Authentically yours,
Ryan Fahey

CAREER, LIFE AND WEALTH BUILDING BOOK RECOMMENDATIONS

The Everyday Hero Manifesto - Robin Sharma
Redefining Realistic - Heather Moyse
10x Is Greater Than 2x - Dr. Benjamin Hardy and Dan Sullivan
Your Best Decade - Ryan Fahey
Greenlights - Matthew McConaughey
The Earned Life - Marshall Goldsmith
The Compound Effect - Darren Hardy

ENDNOTES

Chapter 1
1. Chandler, A. (2023, January 30). *A history of the drive-thru, from California to Coronavirus.* Serious Eats. https://www.seriouseats.com/drive-thru-history#:~:text=But%20it%20wasn%27t%20until,in%20restaurants%20started%20to%20decline
2. Editors of Encyclopaedia Britannica. (2022, August 8). *Breakfast cereal.* Britannica. https://www.britannica.com/topic/breakfast-cereal

Chapter 2
1. Hallman, S., LeVasseur, S., Bérard-Chagnon, J., & Martel, L. (2022, April 27). *A portrait of Canada's growing population aged 85 and older from the 2021 Census.* Statistics Canada. https://www12.statcan.gc.ca/census-recensement/2021/as-sa/98-200-X/2021004/98-200-x20210 04-eng.cfm
2. Canadian Institute for Health Information. (n.d.). *Canada's seniors population outlook: Unchartered territory* [Infographic]. https://www.cihi.ca/en/infographic-canadas-seniors-population-outlook-uncharted-territory
3. Rothenberg, E. (2023, July 29). *You could win free sandwiches for life if you change your name*

to *'Subway'*. CNN Business. https://www.cnn.com/2023/07/29/business-food/subway-name-change-raffle-trnd/index.html
4. Yaghi, M. (2023, April 2). *Farmers wanted: The labour renewal Canada needs to build the Next Green Revolution.* Royal Bank of Canada. https://thoughtleadership.rbc.com/farmers-wanted-the-labour-renewal-canada-needs-to-build-the-next-green-revolution/
5. Statistics Canada. (2022, December 12). *Demographic estimates by age and sex, provinces and territories.* https://www150.statcan.gc.ca/n1/pub/71-607-x/71-607-x2020018-eng.htm
6. Statistics Canada. (2022, December 12). Demographic estimates by age and sex, provinces and territories. https://www150.statcan.gc.ca/n1/pub/71-607-x/71-607-x2020018-eng.htm
7. Joint Center for Housing Studies. (n.d.). *Demographics of an aging America.* Harvard University. https://www.jchs.harvard.edu/sites/default/files/jchs-housing_americas_older_adults_2014-ch2_0.pdf
8. Statistics Canada. (2022, December 12). Demographic estimates by age and sex, provinces and territories. https://www150.statcan.gc.ca/n1/pub/71-607-x/71-607-x2020018-eng.htm
9. O'Neill, A. (2023, May 16). Age distribution in India 2011-2021. Statista. https://www.statista.com/statistics/271315/age-distribution-in-india/#:~:text=In%202021%2C%20about%2025.69%20percent,over%2065%20years%20of%20age.&-

text=India%20is%20one%20of%20the,its%20population%20is%20constantly%20increasing

10. Orlando, J. (2023, January 26). The greying of Canada's population. TD Economics. https://economics.td.com/ca-demographics
11. Gamrot, S. (2022, July 6). The work from home trend is crushing Toronto's office occupancy rates. blogTO.https://www.blogto.com/real-estate-toronto/2022/07/work-from-home-toronto-office-occupancy-rat e/
12. McCourt, C. (Host). (2022, December 13). From sales to CEO + How side hustles are changing the employee game: Interview w/Jeff Dolan, CEO Wavve [Audio podcast episode]. In Fearless Future with Catherine McCourt. iHeart. https://www.iheart.com/podcast/269-fearless-future-w-catherin-81625252/episode/from-sales-ceo-how-105991335/

Chapter 3

1. Hallam, A. (2022). *Balance: How to invest and spend for happiness, health, and wealth.* Friesens.
2. Patterson Neubert, A. (2018, February 13). *Money only buys happiness for a certain amount.* Purdue University. https://www.purdue.edu/newsroom/releases/2018/Q1/money-only-buys-happiness-for-a-certain-a mount.html
3. Charles Schwab. (2023, June). *Charles Schwab modern wealth survey 2023.* https://content.schwab.com/web/retail/public/about-schwab/schwab_modern_wealth_survey_202 3_findings.pdf

Chapter 4

1. Indursky, M. (2017, December 6). *In search of happiness.* HuffPost. https://www.huffpost.com/entry/search-happiness_b_1647207#:~:text=Yes%2C%20there%20are%20more%20than,overwhelming%20number%20of%20them%20are

2. Associated Press. (2020, June 16). *Americans are the unhappiest they've been in 50 years, poll finds.* NBC News.https://www.nbcnews.com/politics/politics-news/americans-are-unhappiest-they-ve-been-50-years-poll-finds-n1231153

3. Clear, J. [@JamesClear]. (2019, May 25). *Commitment devices – Any choice in the present that locks in future behavior* [Tweet]. Twitter. https://twitter.com/JamesClear/status/1132455517094199297

4. Market.Us. (2023, March 14). *Corporate wellness market to cross to USD 100.8 billion in revenues by 2032, at CAGR 6.1%.* GlobeNewswire. https://www.globenewswire.com/en/news-release/2023/03/14/2626815/0/en/Corporate-Wellness-Market-to-Cross-to-USD-100-8-Billion-in-Revenues-by-2032-At-CAGR-6-1.html

Chapter 5

1. Chang, C. H. (2023, May 17). *Selling ethically + manipulative sales tactics to avoid.* LinkedIn. https://www.linkedin.com/pulse/selling-ethically-manipulative-sales-tactics-avoid-chin-hing-chang 2. Smith, W. (2021). *Will* (p. 233). Penguin Press.

2. Communication Theory. (2023, August 7). *The Johari Window Model*. Retrieved August 7, 2023, from https://www.communicationtheory.org/the-johari-window-model/

Chapter 6

1. Obama, B. (2020). *A promised land*. Crown.
2. History.com Editors. (2023, March 29). *Nelson Mandela released from prison*. HISTORY. https://www.history.com/this-day-in-history/nelson-mandela-released-from-prison

Chapter 8

1. MasterClass. (2022, August 31). *Reflective thinking: How to practice reflective thinking*. https://www.masterclass.com/articles/reflective-thinking
2. Clifford, C. (2019, July 28). *Bill Gates took solo 'think weeks' in a cabin in the woods – why it's a great strategy*. CNBC Make It. https://www.cnbc.com/2019/07/26/bill-gates-took-solo-think-weeks-in-a-cabin-in-the-woods.html

Chapter 9

1. Thier, J. (2022, April 27). *This year's college grads think they'll earn over $100,000 from their first job*. Fortune. https://fortune.com/2022/04/27/college-grad-salaries-expectations-reality/ 2. Sullivan, D., & Hardy, B. (2023). *10x is easier than 2x: How world-class entrepreneurs achieve more by doing less*. Hay House, Inc.

2. Rosen, J. (2008, May 26). *Return to paradise: The enduring relevance of John Milton*. The New Yorker. https://www.newyorker.com/magazine/2008/06/02/return-to-paradise
3. Fahey, R. (2019, February 17). *Why we need to be 'ok' in the fallow season: How struggle can breed growth*. Medium. https://medium.com/swlh/why-we-need-to-be-ok-in-the-fallow-season-1d049d4e6d05

Chapter 10

1. Dictionary.com. (n.d.). Catch lightning in a bottle. Retrieved July 24, 2023, from https://www.dictionary.com/browse/catch-lightning-in-a-bottle#:~:text=to%20accomplish%20some thing%20extraordinarily%20difficult,bottle%20to%20make%20the%20playoffs
2. Petriello, M. (2019, September 27). *9 reasons why October baseball is different*. MLB. https://www.mlb.com/news/what-really-changes-in-october-baseball
3. Pinto, G. (2012, October 23). *The 10 worst MLB teams ever to win the World Series*. Bleacher Report. https://bleacherreport.com/articles/1379230-the-10-worst-mlb-teams-ever-to-win-the-world-series
4. Bhusan, B. (2016, December 17). The AirBNB story no one believed by Brian Chesky. [Video]. YouTube. https://www.youtube.com/watch?v=vEcACMyz3Rc&t=541s

www.ingramcontent.com/pod-product-compliance
Lightning Source LLC
Chambersburg PA
CBHW021128080526
44587CB00012B/1185